HOW DID
HELEN KELLER
MAKE HISTORY?

JANE SUTCLIFFE

Sandy Creek
NEW YORK

For Eileen

An Imprint of Sterling Publishing
387 Park Avenue South
New York, NY 10016

Text copyright © 2014 by Jane Sutcliffe
Illustrations copyright © 2014 by Lerner Publishing Group, Inc.

This 2014 edition published by Sandy Creek.

Cover photo courtesy of the Library of Congress
Text illustrations by Tad Butler
Cover design by Jo Obarowski

Library of Congress Cataloging-in-Publication Data

Sutcliffe, Jane.
How did Helen Keller make history? / Jane Sutcliffe. — Custom edition.
pages cm.
Includes bibliographical references and index.
ISBN 978–1–4351–5051–5 (pbk. : alk. paper)
1. Keller, Helen, 1880–1968—Juvenile literature. 2. Deafblind women—United
States—Biography—Juvenile literature. I. Sutcliffe, Jane. Helen Keller. II. Title.
HV1624.K4S87 2014
362.4'1092—dc23 [B]   2013038657

Manufactured in China
1 – RRD – 1/1/2014

TABLE OF CONTENTS

INTRODUCTION

Helen Keller could do almost anything. She was a brilliant thinker. She understood several languages. She wrote books and gave speeches all over the world.

There were only two things that Helen could not do. She couldn't see. And she couldn't hear. She never let that stop her. She did what she set out to do just the same.

People were amazed when they saw all that Helen could do, despite all she could not. She showed the world that anyone can have big dreams.

This is her story.

1 THE No-World

Helen Keller discovered words early. She was born on June 27, 1880, in Tuscumbia, a little town in Alabama. Helen was a bright, beautiful child. When she was only six months old, she began to talk. She delighted her parents by saying "tea, tea, tea." She said "wah-wah" for "water."

Helen's father (LEFT) and mother (RIGHT)

Then, when Helen was not yet two, she became very sick. For days, she had a fever. The family doctor told Kate and Arthur Keller that their little girl might die.

One morning, though, the fever suddenly left. At first, the Kellers were overjoyed. Then they realized that something was wrong. When Kate waved her hand before Helen's eyes, she didn't blink. When she rang a dinner bell, Helen didn't seem to hear it.

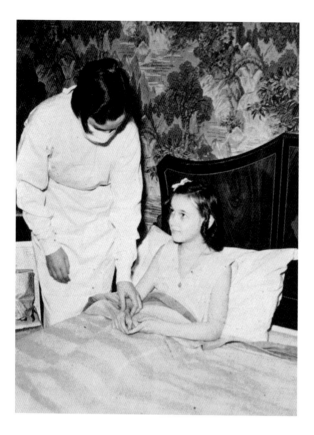

A doctor cares for a girl who is sick. Years after Helen was sick, doctors found better ways to treat dangerous illnesses.

The illness had left Helen blind and deaf. She could no longer see her mother's face or hear her father's voice. Suddenly, she lived in a lonely world of darkness and silence. Later, she called it her "no-world."

Helen could no longer hear words, so she could not learn words. She forgot the few words she had learned as a baby. She remembered only "wah-wah" for "water."

For everything else, she made motions. When she wanted bread, she made the motion of slicing and buttering bread. For her father, she pretended to put on glasses. For her baby sister, she sucked her thumb.

Still, Helen's motions weren't enough. There was so much more that she wanted to say! But without words, she couldn't always make herself understood. Often she exploded in anger. She kicked and screamed and cried until she was worn out. Sometimes her tantrums went on all day.

Deaf children are taught sign language so they can speak through motions. Young Helen used her own signs.

Her parents didn't have the heart to punish her. Instead, Helen was allowed to do pretty much as she pleased. At meals, she grabbed food from other people's plates. She threw dishes and lamps. Once she locked her mother in the pantry. Another time, she pinched her grandmother.

Helen was becoming wild. Her parents knew they had to find a way to help her. They took her to one doctor after another. The answer was always the same. No one could help Helen see or hear again.

Doctors treated many patients with ear and eye problems in the late 1800s. But they could not help Helen.

When Helen was six, her parents took her to a doctor in Baltimore, Maryland. The man agreed that Helen could not be cured. But he had an idea. She could be taught, he said. He gave them the name of a man in Washington, D.C., who might help.

The man's name was Dr. Alexander Graham Bell. Dr. Bell was famous for inventing the telephone. But he was also a well-known teacher of deaf people. The Kellers went to Washington at once.

Alexander Graham Bell helped deaf children learn to speak. Helen's parents hoped he could help her too.

Right away, Helen loved Dr. Bell. He seemed to understand all her signs. She sat on his lap and played with his watch.

Dr. Bell's words gave the Kellers hope at last. He told them to write to the Perkins Institution for the Blind in Boston, Massachusetts. That's where they might find someone to teach Helen, he said.

Mr. Keller wrote immediately. Before long, an answer came back. The school would send a teacher. Her name was Annie Sullivan. She would help Helen find a way out of her no-world.

"I AM GLAD TO WRITE YOU A LETTER"

Helen did not forget Dr. Bell's kindness. Once she had learned how to write, she sent many letters to her new friend. The first one, written in 1887, began, "I am glad to write you a letter." And Dr. Bell was pleased to write to Helen. Their letters continued back and forth for many years.

2 TEACHER

March 3, 1887, would turn out to be the most important day in Helen's life. But six-year-old Helen didn't know that. She knew only that something special was happening in the Keller house.

Annie Sullivan had been a student at the Perkins Institution for the Blind. She was only twenty when she came to teach Helen.

She could feel people hurrying here and there. She stood on the porch steps and waited. Suddenly, she felt footsteps approaching. Her teacher, Annie Sullivan, had arrived.

Helen wasn't so sure she wanted Annie there. She was used to having her own way. She fought Annie. Once she struck Annie and knocked out a tooth.

But Annie was just as tough as Helen. When Helen tried to snatch food from Annie's plate, Annie stopped her. When Helen threw her spoon to the floor, Annie took Helen's hand and made her pick it up. Slowly, Helen began to obey her new teacher.

While Annie taught Helen about manners, she was also teaching her about words. She used a special finger alphabet for deaf people. Her fingers formed a different shape for each letter. Helen felt each letter shape with her hand. Annie gave Helen a doll and spelled *D-O-L-L* with her fingers. She gave her some cake and spelled *C-A-K-E.*

DOLL was the first word Helen learned to spell.

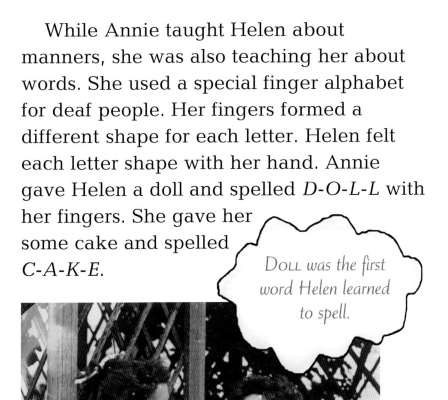

Helen around the age of seven

For weeks, Annie spelled words for Helen. Helen was quick to imitate Annie's finger movements. But she didn't know she was spelling words. To her, it was all a game. She even tried to teach Belle, her dog, to spell with her paw. Belle wasn't interested.

Then one day, Annie took Helen outside. She started pumping water from the well. Helen felt Annie place her hand under the spout. She felt cool water pouring over one hand. In the other hand, she felt Annie's fingers spell *W-A-T-E-R*—slowly, at first, then faster and faster.

The water pump outside Helen's childhood home

Suddenly Helen understood. *W-A-T-E-R* was the cool, wet something spilling into her hand. It had a name!

Everything had a name! Helen was in a hurry to know them all. Annie's fingers spelled word after word for Helen. Then Helen pointed to Annie. *T-E-A-C-H-E-R*, Annie spelled. From then on, that was Helen's name for Annie.

Teacher called Helen "all fingers and curiosity."

After that, Teacher "talked" into Helen's hand nearly all the time. She described everything she saw and heard. Helen didn't understand all the words at first. But she learned quickly. Each new word made her happy. Her wild behavior improved.

Best of all, words gave her a way to learn about the world. Teacher made maps of clay and told her about great mountains and rivers. She handed her a fossil to feel and told her about dinosaurs. She took her for walks in the woods and taught her about nature.

Soon Helen learned to read. Her fingers felt raised letters. Later, she read special books with patterns of raised dots. That kind of writing is called Braille. Her fingers flew as she read.

She learned to write too. She loved to write cheery letters to her friends and family. She sometimes signed them, "From your little friend, Helen A. Keller." (The *A* was for "Adams.") Everyone who read her letters was astonished. Helen had learned so much so fast! The director of the Perkins Institution for the Blind was amazed. He wrote an article about Helen.

Suddenly, little Helen was big news. Reporters began to write about her. Word spread quickly. Soon, people all over the world were talking about her.

Helen used a special board with grooves to write. This kind of writing is called squarehand.

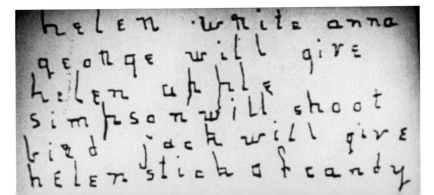

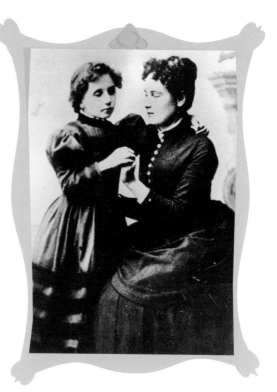

Ten-year-old Helen (LEFT) and Teacher use the finger alphabet to talk.

In May 1888, Helen took a trip. Annie and Mrs. Keller went too. They visited Dr. Bell in Washington, D.C. They met President Grover Cleveland at the White House.

Then they went to Boston to the Perkins Institution. Helen made friends with the students there. She was delighted to find that deaf and blind children there knew the finger alphabet too. At last, she could talk to other children in her own language.

Helen stayed at the school that spring and the next fall, in 1889. While she was there, she started learning French. She learned some Latin and some Greek words too. Soon, she was using the foreign words in her letters. She made almost no mistakes.

Still Helen pleaded to be taught more. "I do want to learn much about everything," she wrote. But that wasn't quite true. Helen wanted to learn *everything* about everything.

WELCOME TO THE CIRCUS, HELEN!

One day, the circus came to town. Helen couldn't see the circus, so she was allowed to feel it instead. She rode an elephant and petted the lion cubs. When a monkey did tricks for the audience, she was allowed to keep her hand on him to "watch."

3 CLASS OF 1904

Helen's hands were always in motion. She used her hands even when she was talking to herself. When Helen was nine, she made a big decision. She wanted to speak with her mouth instead of her hands. She began taking lessons to learn to talk like other people.

It wasn't an easy job. Helen couldn't hear what words were supposed to sound like. She couldn't hear the sounds she made either. She never knew if she was getting the words right. Mostly, she got them wrong.

She did learn to read lips with her fingers. She placed her hand lightly over a speaker's mouth and throat. Then she "listened" to what the person said. But she still had to spell her reply with her fingers.

Helen uses her hand to "hear" what Teacher is saying.

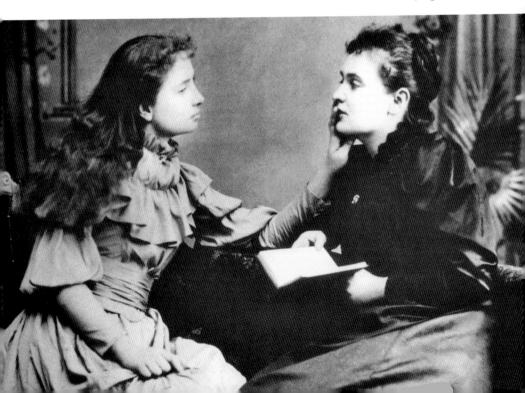

Then Helen and Teacher met two men who were opening a school for deaf children in New York City. The two men felt certain they could help Helen speak clearly. Perhaps she could even learn to sing!

For Helen, this sounded like a dream come true. In October 1894, she became a student at the school. Teacher went with her.

Helen liked New York. She liked her studies too, especially her classes in German. The only subject she didn't like was math. She had a bad habit of guessing at the answer instead of working it out. Still, she worked hard.

Helen poses in her class picture at the school for deaf children. Helen sits in the front row, FAR LEFT, holding Teacher's hand.

She worked hardest at her speaking lessons. "Oh . . . how I should like to speak like other people," she wrote to a friend. She was willing to work day and night, she said. But her hard work wasn't enough. Her words still were not clear.

Once, when she was little, Helen told friends she wanted to go to college. It was a surprising dream. At that time, few girls went to college. For Helen, it seemed impossible. But Helen was used to doing what everyone else thought impossible.

A GOOD MEMORY AND A SAD TALE

When Helen was eleven, she wrote a story called "The Frost King." The story was printed in a magazine. Then came terrible news. Her story had really been written by someone else. A friend had read the story to Helen years before. Helen did not recall hearing the story. But somehow she had remembered it clearly. She wrote in her journal, "My heart was full of tears."

A person reads a Braille book. When Helen was in school, many of her books were not in Braille.

In 1896, sixteen-year-old Helen entered the Cambridge School for Young Ladies. Her studies there would help her get ready for college. For the first time, she was in classes with students who could see and hear. Teacher went to all her classes with her. She sat by Helen's side and spelled the lessons into her hand. Most of Helen's books were not printed in Braille. Teacher spelled those too.

It was a lot of work for both Helen and Teacher. Even so, Helen made amazing progress. She passed all her exams, many with honors.

In September 1900, Helen entered Radcliffe College. She was already famous. But this time, she was making history. She was the first deaf-blind person ever to go to college. To welcome Helen, her classmates gave her a Boston terrier as a present. She named the dog Phiz.

Helen plunged right into her studies. She took classes in French, German, history, English, and more. Her best subject was

writing. And her best stories were the ones she wrote about her own life. Her stories were beautiful, funny, and full of joy.

Teacher reads to Helen by spelling words into her hand. Phiz lies by Helen's feet in this photo.

Other people heard about Helen's stories. They urged her to turn them into a book. In 1903, Helen's book, *The Story of My Life*, was published. She dedicated it to her good friend, Alexander Graham Bell.

At last, on a June day in 1904, Helen sat with ninety-six other women. Ninety-five of them were her classmates. The other was Annie Sullivan. With her teacher by her side, Helen received her college degree, with honors. At twenty-four, Helen Keller was a college graduate.

Helen wore a cap and gown for her graduation from Radcliffe College.

4 INTRODUCING HELEN KELLER

Helen had spent nearly her whole life learning. It was time to do something with what she'd learned. She had told Dr. Bell once that she wanted to be a writer. She had already written one book. She decided she would keep writing.

Helen (SEATED) with John Macy and Annie

Helen and Annie moved into a big farmhouse in Massachusetts. Soon Annie's husband, John Macy, joined them. (They married in 1905). John helped Helen with her writing.

In 1908, Helen's second book, *The World I Live In*, was published. Helen knew that most people could not even imagine what it was like to be blind and deaf. So she told them. She described how she experienced the world, especially through touch. "My hand is to me what your hearing and sight together are to you," she wrote.

Readers loved the book. They were curious about Helen's dark, silent world. They would never tire of reading about her life.

Helen wanted to write about more than just her life, though. She wanted to write about her ideas.

Helen had strong opinions about how the country should be run. She believed that owning private property was a bad idea. Instead, she believed, everything should be shared equally by all. (That idea is called socialism.)

In Helen's day, women were not allowed to vote. She thought that was wrong too. She marched in parades to show her support for women's rights.

Helen marched in this 1913 parade in Washington, D.C. The parade was in support of women's right to vote.

Books that Helen read helped her form her opinions and ideas.

Many people frowned at Helen's ideas. Some even said that because she was blind and deaf, she didn't know any better. That made Helen angry. She invited people to attack her ideas. But she felt it wasn't "fair fighting" to remind people that she couldn't see or hear. After all, she could still think and read.

Helen also had opinions about how to help blind people. The government should do more, she argued. The blind needed more education and more jobs. They needed more Braille books. Helen wrote articles and visited schools to help.

She wanted to do more. She wanted to speak at meetings and in lectures. To do that, she would have to improve her speech. Once more Helen worked hard to learn to talk. She took lessons from a singing teacher. Slowly her voice grew stronger. Her words became clearer.

Helen spoke out about the need for Braille books. Here, volunteers for the Red Cross help create Braille versions of printed books.

Helen and Teacher began giving lectures. They spoke all over North America. Teacher told the audience how she had taught Helen about words. Then it was Helen's turn. How proud she was of her accomplishment! Wherever they went, Helen and Teacher were greeted with cheers and applause.

Helen (LEFT) gets ready to board a plane. Helen and Teacher traveled across the United States giving lectures.

Helen met President Calvin Coolidge at the White House in 1926. She had become so famous that she met nearly every U.S. president of her time.

Helen's words always gave hope to blind people. But Helen knew the blind needed more than hope. They needed help. In 1924, she began speaking to raise money for the American Foundation for the Blind. She spoke in homes, in churches, and at meetings. People flocked to see the famous Helen Keller. When she asked them to donate money, they did. "Purses Fly Open to Helen Keller," read one headline.

I'M JUST HERE FOR THE SEALS

For a while, Helen and Teacher spoke in theaters. Their "act" was sandwiched in among all kinds of others. They might follow a famous singer, a man on stilts, or a pack of trained seals.

With Teacher, Helen spoke to thousands of people in hundreds of cities across the country. In 1930, at the age of forty-nine, she spoke before the U.S. Congress. She wanted the government to help provide more Braille books for the blind. Soon after, the idea became law.

Helen was busier than ever. She was excited about her work for the blind. But Annie was tired. She was often sick. On October 20, 1936, at the age of seventy, she died. Helen held her hand as Teacher took her last breath. It was the same hand that had first spelled words to her as a little girl.

Nearly all her life, Teacher had been by her side. At fifty-six, Helen would have to go on without her.

5 AFTER TEACHER

Polly Thompson had been Helen's assistant for many years. She lived and traveled with Helen after Teacher's death. But no one could really take Teacher's place.

Helen missed Teacher. But there was work to do. She had already done so much to help blind people in the United States. She wanted to do the same for the blind in other countries.

In 1937, Helen and Polly traveled to Japan. Helen was to raise money for blind and deaf people there. People must have been very eager to hear what Helen had to say. She gave ninety-seven speeches in thirty-nine cities.

The Japanese people greeted Helen like a star. Children lined the streets to see her. They waved flags and shouted her name. Her trip was a tremendous success.

THE DOG LOVER

Helen had always loved dogs. On her trip to Japan, she was given a puppy as a gift. The dog was an Akita, a favorite breed in Japan. When Helen took her puppy home with her, it became the first Akita dog in the United States.

Then, just a few years later, on December 7, 1941, there was startling news. Japanese planes attacked U.S. ships at Pearl Harbor, Hawaii.

Suddenly, the United States was at war. Soldiers were being wounded on battlefields. Many had become blind or deaf. Helen visited hospitals. She held soldiers' hands and gave them words of encouragement. Most of all, she showed them that living without sight or hearing did not mean living without hope.

Helen (CENTER) and Polly (RIGHT) visit a soldier wounded during World War II.

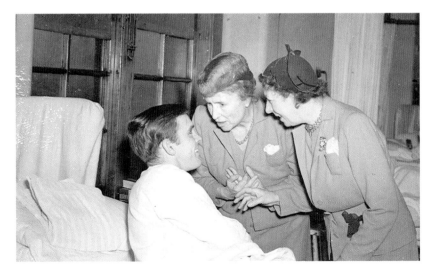

By the end of the war, Helen was sixty-five years old. Many people began to slow down at that age. Not Helen. "Life is either a daring adventure or nothing," she once said. And she was ready for adventure.

With Polly by her side, Helen traveled the world. She took her fight for the blind to thirty-five other countries. She spoke at universities and hospitals. She met with presidents, kings, and queens. She received honors and awards wherever she went.

Polly (LEFT) helps Helen (CENTER) put on a sari, an Indian dress, for an event in India.

First Lady Eleanor Roosevelt (LEFT) speaks with Helen.
Mrs. Roosevelt praised Helen's work overseas.

Over and over, Helen spoke to cheering
crowds. Over and over, she urged people to
find ways to help the blind help themselves.
Over and over, her words brought hope to
the blind.

Helen had not forgotten about writing.
In 1954, at the age of seventy-four, she
completed a new book. *Teacher* was written
to honor her teacher, Annie Sullivan. Helen
had never stopped missing Teacher. She
gave credit to Teacher for all she had
accomplished in her life. "People think
Teacher has left me," she told a friend, "but
she is with me all the time."

Helen with her 1955 Academy Award for HELEN KELLER, IN HER STORY

These were busy years for Helen. She appeared in a movie about her life. The movie later went on to win an Academy Award. And in 1955, she left for a lengthy tour through Asia. She traveled forty thousand miles in five months. She was seventy-five.

It was time for Helen to slow down at last. She was happy to stay at her home in Connecticut. (She had moved there many years before.) She surrounded herself with books. She read and studied. She told friends she wanted to learn new languages. "I shall devote my old age to study," she said. She still had not lost her hunger for learning.

In 1964, Helen was awarded the Presidential Medal of Freedom. It is the nation's highest honor for civilians. But Helen was too ill and frail to receive the medal in person.

On June 1, 1968, Helen died. It was just weeks before her eighty-eighth birthday. She was one of the most famous women in the world. People everywhere knew the story of Helen's life.

Many people had felt sorry for Helen. They thought she must have lived a life filled with silence and darkness. But those people were wrong. Helen had lived a life filled with friends and adventure. She had lived a life filled with joy.

TIMELINE

HELEN KELLER WAS BORN ON JUNE 27, 1880, IN TUSCUMBIA, ALABAMA.

In the year . . .

1882   Helen became blind and deaf after an illness.

1886   she met Dr. Alexander Graham Bell.

1887   Annie Sullivan came to Tuscumbia and began teaching Helen.   Age 6

1894   she attended a school for the deaf in New York.

1896   she attended the Cambridge School for Young Ladies.   Age 16

1900   she entered Radcliffe College.

1903   her first book, *The Story of My Life*, was published.

1904   she received a degree from Radcliffe and became the first deaf-blind person to graduate from college.   Age 24

1908   *The World I Live In* was published.

1913   she began giving lectures with Annie Sullivan.

1924   she began her work for the American Foundation for the Blind.   Age 44

1936   Annie Sullivan died.

1937   Helen traveled to Japan.

1946   she made her first world tour to speak on behalf of the blind.   Age 66

1955   *Teacher*, her book about Annie Sullivan, was published.

1964   she was awarded the Presidential Medal of Freedom from President Lyndon Johnson.   Age 84

1968   she died on June 1.   Age 87

A VISIT TO IVY GREEN

The house where Helen grew up was called Ivy Green. In 1954, it became a memorial to Helen Keller.

Every year, people visit Ivy Green. They come to see the cottage where Helen was born. They see the porch where she first met Annie Sullivan. They touch the black well pump in the garden.

Each summer, a famous play is performed there. *The Miracle Worker* tells the story of Annie's struggle to teach the wild young Helen. And it shows the "miracle" that happened at that pump. People come to watch Helen's story. They see that miracle happen right where it happened for Helen—Ivy Green.

Helen was born in this cottage, across from the main house at Ivy Green.

FURTHER READING

Alexander, Sally Hobart, and Robert Alexander. *She Touched the World: Laura Bridgman, Deaf-Blind Pioneer.* Boston: Houghton Mifflin Harcourt, 2008. Read about Laura Bridgman, another deaf and blind child who overcame countless obstacles in the 1840s.

Donaldson, Madeline. *Louis Braille.* Minneapolis: Lerner Publications Company, 2007. Read about the young Frenchman who, at the age of fifteen, invented an alphabet of raised dots for the blind.

McPherson, Stephanie Sammartino. *Alexander Graham Bell.* Minneapolis: Lerner Publications Company, 2007. Learn about the famous inventor of the telephone, teacher of the deaf, and Helen's friend.

SELECT BIBLIOGRAPHY

Herrmann, Dorothy. *Helen Keller: A Life*. New York: Alfred A. Knopf, 1998.

Keller, Helen. *The Story of My Life*. Garden City, NY: Doubleday, 1954.

Keller, Helen. *Teacher: Anne Sullivan Macy*. Westport, CT: Greenwood Press, 1985. First published 1955 by Doubleday.

Keller, Helen. *To Love This Life: Quotations by Helen Keller*. New York: AFB Press, 2000.

Keller, Helen. *The World I Live In*. New York: Century Co., 1908.

Lash, Joseph P. *Helen and Teacher: The Story of Helen Keller and Anne Sullivan Macy*. New York: Delacorte Press, 1980.

Nielsen, Kim. *The Radical Lives of Helen Keller*. New York: NYU Press, 2004.

INDEX

Acknowledgments

For photographs: The images in this book are used with the permission of: © Bettmann/CORBIS, pp. 4, 26, 27, 40, 41, 43; © Walter Sanders/Time Life Pictures/Getty Images, pp. 7, 19; Courtesy of the National Library of Medicine, p. 8; © CAROLING LEE/ZUMA Press, p. 9; The Granger Collection, New York, p. 10; © SSPL/The Image Works, p. 11; Courtesy of Perkins School for the Blind, Watertown, MA, pp. 14, 20, 38, 39; Thaxter Parks Spencer Papers, R. Stanton Avery Special Collections Department, New England Historic Genealogical Society, Boston, MA., p. 15; © The Toronto Star/ZUMA Press, p. 16; Courtesy of the American Foundation for the Blind, Helen Keller Archives, pp. 17, 24, 28, 30, 35, 42; Courtesy Everett Collection, pp. 18, 23; Library of Congress, pp. 31 (LC-DIG-ggbain-11365), 32 (LC-USZ62-68305), 45 (HABS ALA,17-TUSM, 4-4); © CORBIS, p. 33; © Roger-Viollet/The Image Works, p. 34. Front cover: Library of Congress. **For quoted material:** p. 12, Helen Keller, *The Story of My Life* (Garden City, NY: Doubleday, 1954), 288; p. 18, Dorothy Herrmann, *Helen Keller: A Life* (New York: Alfred A. Knopf, 1998), 56; p. 19, Hermann, 73; p. 21, Joseph P. Lash, *Helen and Teacher: The Story of Helen Keller and Anne Sullivan Macy* (New York: Delacorte Press, 1980), 93; p. 25, Keller, *The Story of My Life*, 344; p. 25, Lash, 134; p. 30, Helen Keller, *The World I Live In* (New York: Century Co., 1908), 5; p. 32, Kim Nielsen, *The Radical Lives of Helen Keller* (New York: NYU Press, 2004), 49; p. 35, Lash, 530; p. 40, Helen Keller, *To Love This Life* (New York: AFB Press, 2000), 35; p. 40, Hermann, 271; p. 41, Helen Keller, *Teacher: Anne Sullivan Macy* (Westport, CT: Greenwood Press, 1985, originally published 1955 by Doubleday), 23; p. 42, Herrmann, 308.